INTRODUCTION

The American stencil era, from 1775 to around 1860, was the period in which stenciling as a form of interior decoration was most popular. New England and Pennsylvania developed their own regional characteristic styles. Extensive collections of Pennsylvania Dutch folk art have been preserved over the years by museums and private persons. They constitute part of our rich American heritage and culture. While much of Pennsylvania Dutch folk decoration is, in fact, hand painted, this book has adapted many designs into stencil form. Using these stencils, anyone can easily reproduce the hand-painted designs precisely with a minimum of effort.

The stencil designs of Pennsylvania reflect the rich heritage of old-world peasant design. The Dutch, German and Swiss immigrants who settled in Pennsylvania brought with them an abundant source of folk decoration from their homelands. In a short time these designs took on the characteristic flavor of what we recognize as Pennsylvania Dutch folk art. The most popular motifs were tulips, hearts, birds of every description, stars, mermaids, animals and fanciful creatures. The Pennsylvania Dutch settlers showed no restraint in their execution of design or choice of color. Their style is bold and strong yet simple and direct. Like all forms of early American folk decoration, their art projected a desire to make their surroundings brighter, gayer and more pleasant. It also reflected contentment with their new way of life and pride in their new home, America.

The Pennsylvania Dutch, like the New Englanders, decorated any object that struck their fancy. Furniture of every description including chairs, chests, picture frames, bedboards, tables, window cornices, doors and boxes of all shapes and sizes were decorated with the graceful patterns of the Pennsylvania Dutch. Tinware, perhaps the most famous medium of Pennsylvania Dutch folk art, was used for fanciful and gaily decorated stove plates, trays, coffeepots, cups, canisters, lampshades and boxes that expressed their maker's love and appreciation for the objects adorned. The Pennsylvania Dutch settlers could not ornament their stone houses with painted designs, so they maintained the decorative tradition by transplanting the idea from the house to the wooden face of their fine barns. Hex symbols and circular geometric designs were painted in bright colors with sharp, clean lines that reflected the neat and orderly life style of these early settlers.

This book is filled with authentic Pennsylvania Dutch stencil designs that can be cut out and used for decorating walls, floors, furniture, fabrics, tin, leather and almost any other surface. All materials needed are inexpensive and easy to find in most well-stocked hardware or art-supply stores. The method is easily mastered and projects quickly completed.

LIST OF MATERIALS

boiled linseed oil
turpentine
rags
stencil knife and blades
knife sharpener or carborundum stone
large knitting needles or ice pick
cutting surface (glass, wood, etc.)

masking tape
paint
textile paint (for fabric)
stenciling brushes
newspaper
fine sandpaper
desk blotters (for fabric)
varnish (for floors, wood, tin)
#4 artists' brush

Stencil knife and two stenciling brushes of different sizes.

First, cut out an entire page (= stencil plate) from the book with a pair of scissors. When more than one design appears on a page, a dotted line serves as the cutting guideline for separating each design onto a distinct stencil plate. The margin of ¾ inch or more around the design makes the stencil sturdy and durable while in use and protects the surrounding areas from paint when stenciling.

The pages of this book are of medium-weight manila paper, which must be treated with oil to make it tough, leathery and impervious to moisture. Oiled manila will become semi-translucent, allowing light to penetrate slightly. A knife blade will cut through an oiled plate more easily. The oiling process takes place after the plate (page) is cut from the book but before the blacked-in areas of the design are cut out, so there will be no chance of bending or ripping delicate ties (bridge areas) when applying the oil.

A mixture of 50% *boiled* linseed oil and 50% turpentine is applied with a rag to both sides of the plate until it is thoroughly saturated. Using a thumbtack, the plate is then hung to dry. It will dry to the touch in about 10 minutes. Any excess can be wiped off with a dry rag or the plate can be allowed to dry for a longer period. The rag should then be immersed in water until it can be incinerated or removed by regular garbage disposal service. Spontaneous combustion can occur if the rag is stored for later use.

The stencil knife is used for cutting out the small pieces through which the paint will reach the surface to be decorated. Only the solid black areas of each design are cut out. Suitable cutting surfaces for this task are hard wood, a piece of plate glass with the edges taped, or a stack of old newspapers. The oiled stencil plate is placed on the cutting surface and allowed to move freely. Grasp the stencil knife as you would a pencil. Apply even pressure for the entire length of a curve or line. Frequent lifting of the knife causes jagged, uneven edges. The small details of the stencil design are cut out first and larger areas last to prevent weakening the plate before cutting is completed. Sharpen the blade frequently on a carborundum stone or knife sharpener.

Cutting requires careful and accurate work. A jagged line or ragged corner will stencil exactly that way in every impression of the stencil plate.

The narrow bridges of paper between the cut-out areas in the design are known as ties. If you accidentally cut through a tie, apply tape to both sides of the tear and replace the tape when needed. Circles and small dots are difficult to cut with a knife. Various large needles can be used to punch out the circles. Ice picks and different-size knitting needles work well. Carefully use the knife or a small piece of fine sandpaper to trim and smooth the edges.

Paints used for stenciling can be water-base or turpentine-base. Any paint used must be mixed to a fairly thick consistency. Acrylic paint is an excellent water-base paint because it is fast-drying and easy to clean up. Acrylics are sold in tubes or jars and come in the right consistency for stenciling. Japan paints come in small 8-oz. cans and must be thinned slightly with turpentine. Turpentine-base paints must be allowed to dry for 24 hours. Both acrylic and japan paint dry to a flat finish. As soon as stenciling is completed, brushes are cleaned, using water for water-base paints and turpentine for oil or turpentine-base paints.

Stenciling on fabrics requires textile paints or inks made especially for decorating on fabric. Textile paints and inks come either water- or turpentine-soluble and are mixed thinner than regular paints. The fabric must be prewashed or drycleaned to remove any sizing and allow for shrinkage. Blotters must be used underneath the fabric to absorb excess moisture and paint. After the stenciled fabric has dried, ironing will set the textile paint or ink and make the colors permanent and washable. All these coloring mediums can be purchased at an art-supply store.

Brushes used for stenciling are cylindrical. The bristles are cut all the same length, forming a circular flat surface of bristle ends. Stencil brushes come in various sizes. A good selection of sizes would be ¼ inch in diameter, ½ inch in diameter, and 1 inch in diameter. A clean brush is used each time a new color is introduced.

Stenciling begins by securing the stencil plate on two sides with masking tape to the object being stenciled. If the plate is not secure, the action of the stencil brush will cause the design to smear. The brush is grasped like a pencil but held perpendicular to the work surface. Dip only the flat bottom of the bristles into the paint. Do not overload the brush with paint, or it will run under the plate and ruin the design. Have several sheets of newspaper nearby for pouncing out the freshly loaded brush. Pouncing is a hammerlike movement that disperses the paint throughout the bristles. When an even speckling of paint is evident on the newspaper, the brush is ready for use. Stippling is the proper term for the rapid up-and-down motion of the brush over the stencil plate. Stippling continues until the openings in the plate are completely filled in with color.

Several plates in this book have two parts for stenciling in more than one color. The A-plate is stenciled first, and when the paint is dry the B-plate is transferred over the matching parts of the A-stencil. Remember that only the solid black areas of the B-plate design are cut out. Small details from the A-plate design will show when the B-plate is superimposed. These details will enable the stenciler to line up the B-plate correctly.

Masking tape is used to keep different colors clean and separate if you desire to use more than one color for a single stencil plate. The varying parts of the design are masked with tape as each color is transferred. Changing the masking tape is done without removing the plate from the project being stenciled.

The border designs in this book run continuously. On the right or left side of the stencil plate is a portion of the design that is repeated exactly on the opposite side. With each new setting, the design is lined up over its matching place in the previous impression. In this manner the border can run to any length neatly and in a straight line.

Very often the Pennsylvania Dutch used a design and then reversed it to produce a mirror image. Any plate facing right or left in this book can be stenciled facing the opposite way by turning over the stencil plate and stenciling on the back side. When this is done the paint must be carefully and thoroughly cleaned off the side stenciled first so that when the mirror image is stenciled no paint is transferred from the underside of the plate. The paint is removed from the first side with a rag dampened in water or turpentine and allowed to dry completely.

As soon as stenciling with any plate is finished, the plate is wiped gently with a rag or sponge dampened with water or turpentine depending on the paint in use. This increases the life expectancy of the stencil plate by helping prevent the accumulation of paint around the edges of the design.

Certain colors are distinctly Pennsylvania Dutch. Vegetable juices, earth minerals, and soot limited the range of hues that early decorators used. Bright scarlet to dull brown-red, bright yellow to ochre, bright blue, blue-greens, grass green, dull green, earth browns and antique white completed the Pennsylvania Dutch palette. The cover illustrations will give a good idea of the color range.

When mixing colors for stenciling, the addition of raw umber will grey any color and simulate the appearance of age. After stenciling a design, take a #4 artists' brush and polka-dot or stripe it with straight or wavy lines in a contrasting color to enhance the design and make it even more colorful. Sanding the stenciled design with fine sandpaper will make it appear worn. Stencilwork on floors, woodwork, and tin should be protected with several coats of a good varnish.

A more detailed and specific account of the art of stenciling is contained in *The Complete Book of Stencilcraft* (Simon & Schuster), by the author of this book.

6

7

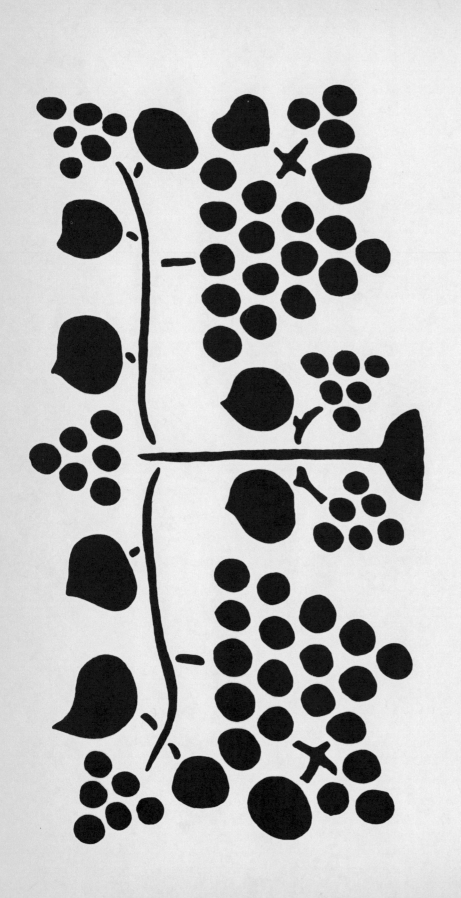

16

17

22

23

24

26

27

28

29

34

Cut out black areas only.

41A

Cut out black areas only.

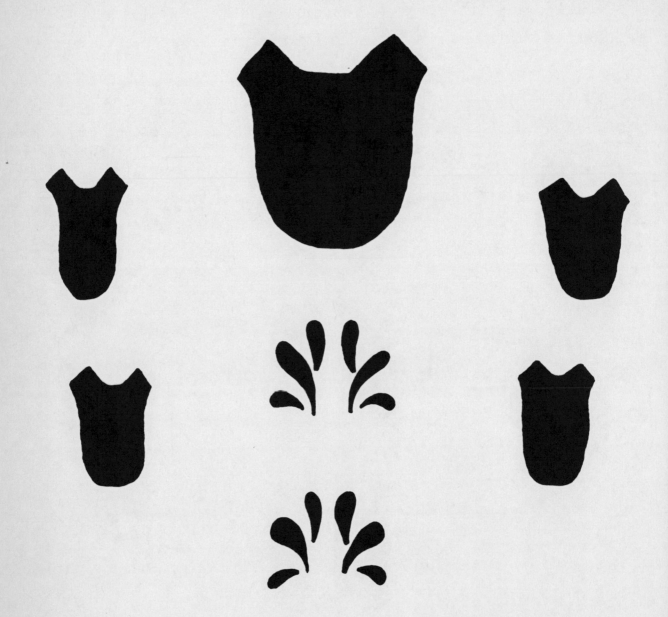